American Creek

This is an IndieMosh book

brought to you by MoshPit Publishing
an imprint of Mosher's Business Support Pty Ltd

PO Box 4363
Penrith NSW 2750

indiemosh.com.au

Copyright © Catherine Harford 2022

The moral right of the author has been asserted in accordance with the Copyright Amendment (Moral Rights) Act 2000.

All rights reserved. Except as permitted under the Australian Copyright Act 1968 (for example, fair dealing for the purposes of study, research, criticism or review) no part of this publication may be reproduced, stored in a retrieval system, or transmitted in any form or by any means, electronic, mechanical, photocopying, recording or otherwise, without the written permission of the publisher.

A catalogue record for this work is available from the National Library of Australia

https://www.nla.gov.au/collections

Title: American Creek

Subtitle: A Collection of Poems

Author: Harford, Catherine (1976–)

ISBNs: 9781922812735 (paperback)

Subjects: LANGUAGE ARTS & DISCIPLINES/Writing/Poetry; ART/Australian & Oceanian; BODY, MIND & SPIRIT/Sacred Sexuality; Angels & Spirit Guides; Paganism & Neo-Paganism

No individual in these poems is taken from real life. Any resemblance to any person or persons living or dead is accidental and unintentional. The author, their agents and publishers cannot be held responsible for any claim otherwise and take no responsibility for any such coincidence.

Cover concept by Catherine Harford.
Cover Artwork: *Sunset in NSW, 1865,* Eugene Von Guérard 1811-1901
Mitchell Library, State Library of New South Wales

The Silent Scream by Catherine Harford

Cover layout by Ally Mosher at allymosher.com

The Silent Scream

Also by Catherine Harford:

They Gave Me Truth
Under Moon and Sun

American Creek

A Collection of Poems

By
CATHERINE HARFORD

*For Frank and Kel
Thanks for all of the laughter
Love and inspiration*

Contents

Introduction 1

One Dream Closer to Love

Desert Dreaming 9
    Karma in Advance 10
    The Quest 12
    The Lost Love of Science 14
    Love's Equation 15
    Fire Dancing 16
    Bevy of Brunettes 18
    My Jugular 19
    Prayer for the Unborn 20
    Kind Folk 22
    Everflow 23
    Seven Towers 24
    Just For You 25
    Reverie 26
    Stay 28
    Lovers 29
    Spirits of a Kind 30
    The Great Mother 32
    A Poem for Frank and Kel 33
    Angel Girl 34
    Wild Australia 35
    The Fondu of Time 36
    Tethered 37
    The Finke 38
    The Boy 39

Dream Big 40

One Step Forward, Two Steps Back

The Emotional Void 45

The Fundamental Crusade.. 46

Old Sydney Town 48

The Saming...50

What am I Holding Onto?... 51

Love and Devotion 52

The Frenemy...54

Shoulders to Cry On 56

The Fool...58

The Lonely Witch..65

The Love We Share 66

Crush the Patriarchy..67

Jealous Tongues.. 68

The Unholy Nuisance 70

The Wall 71

Red and Blue 72

The Judge 73

Faith 74

Are You the One?..76

Wander and Fade 78

Icy, Soulless Day... 80

Katherine..82

The Survivors..83

Time is Up.. 84

One Night Closer to Death

Present Tense 89

Winter Blues 90

Terra Karma	91
Tears in My Soup	92
Samsara Now	94
Paradise Lost	96
Tremulous Truths	98
I Was Meant for Bigger Things	101
Afterlife	102
For Nan	105
Sundancer	108
Fortuna	110
The Emptiness	111
Seven Year Itch	112
The Incessant Sin	113
Balance Restored	114
That Which You Bring to the Party	115
Running Out of Time	116
There's More to Come	117
The Grass is Greener	120
Set Me Free	125
The Grieving	126
The Twilight of Loneliness	128
The Witch from Oz	129
Sheep	130
The Void	131

One Prayer Closer to Awake

The Lightest Prayer	135
Hidden Colour City	136
The Millennial Arrangement	138
Wanderlust	139

At Our Suggestion	140
You're Family Now	142
Made of Stars	145
Psychic Sway	146
A Prayer for Claire	148
The One's Who	150
All I Ask	152
Pepe	154
Leaving Home	158
The Mystery	159
Burn Anew	160
The Lucky Country?	162
Like a Prayer	163
The Artist's Movement	164
The Cautious Cancer	167
Don't Look Back	168
The Running Show	170
The Baptism	172
The Wait	173
American Creek	174
The Traveller	176
Acknowledgements	177
About the Author	180

Introduction

This is my second volume of poetry to be published, and though a collection of poems is relatively self-explanatory, I wanted to take the opportunity to briefly reflect on how it is I approach my particular style of work.

I have had many conversations throughout my life as to what constitutes poetry, and as such, have consequently had many an argument as to what constitutes a "poem."

Traditionally speaking, I'm well aware of the rhyming and the metering that, for most, is the utmost definition of poetry, and that anything less is relegated to that strange, unfettered space of "prose." When I have shown people what I consider to be a poem of mine, at times they have quelled my lofty ambitions, "No no, that doesn't rhyme and doesn't have precise metering, it's actually prose."

Having said this, surely there are enough beatnik or surrealist poets of recent decades whose work flies in the face of tradition to the point of undoing the mould? I'd like to think so, yet it has been a funny little reality to see and hear poets forcing a stanza, determining that the last word of a line must marry up to a rhyming in the following or alternate line, all in the pursuit of what is technically to be considered an actual piece of poetry.

By whatever chance elsewise that I deviated from this traditional path, I did it very early on. I had dabbled in writing poetry, but it didn't really gain traction until I began travelling around Australia (at age 23) in earnest, and found myself so absolutely full to the brim with inspiration that poems began pouring out of me at will.

No doubt there was a punk element to this that coaxed me in my media-arts trained brain to deliberately try to buck the system, to do something different and stuff what anyone thought – which, when you think about it, is almost key in the bid to survive and thrive as an artist in this cutthroat, modern expanse of creative producers. Especially in Australia, where the arts are acknowledged but culturally diminished in favour of sports and, well, anything else that generates extreme wealth – the good old "Lucky Country" doesn't feel all that lucky these days with spiralling house prices and homelessness through the roof, not to mention just a lack of affordability in general day-to-day living. The idea that any artist, poet, writer living in this country might actually make a living off of their art feels like a pipe dream.

Therefore, the need to stand out amongst the crowd is virtually critical to your survival. And while I acknowledge that, early on in my post-university thinking this was an initial consideration, the entire evolution of my work was far more organic and far less calculating.

Besides, I am yet to "survive" on an income generated from any art that I have made – whilst I have remained a practicing artist my entire adult life, I have done so with a passionate dedication that has existed outside of streams of income. So that, happily so, my creative work has come to fruition and existed beyond the controlling hand of any outside, managerial dominion that would seek to determine the financial relativity of my heartfelt creative output, and therefore try to control the content or interfere with my vision.

If anyone reading this has read my first book, "They Gave Me Truth," then the sudden interjection of spiritual mediumship into this discussion will hopefully resonate with understanding. The fact is, as I became more active as a poet, I did so with clear instruction and guidance from the spiritual realm.

As much as I could sit, write and skite here and now about my abilities as a wordsmith, or an artist for that matter, I first and foremost pay homage to these spiritual guides of mine that fuel all of my creative outpourings. They inspire me, invite me into a cosmic dance with them, and before I know it, I have in my hot little hands a piece of art or writing that resounds with much greater significance than anything I might sit and ardently attempt to produce.

If this is difficult to grasp, then, please, if you will, imagine that, just as a psychic does, I act as a medium, and they generate the work through me. Even to the point where I have cockily attempted to alter or "improve" a piece of work, and to my humbled chagrin, have quickly realised it worked better the first time – they bless me with this work, and I embrace it all as that which I am so incredibly lucky to receive.

Initially I had to work hard to reach a certain standard of creative skill, and likewise work on this connection with my gods and guides so that, to simply become a medium at will, I would naturally be able to form this connection – it became second nature, a second skin. Beyond that I learned to abandon my expectations, and to simply embrace the direction they were guiding me in.

To this end, I even found myself arguing the point with them – "Is this really poetry? Isn't it supposed to rhyme a lot more, and be more structured?" Even I, as the artist, poet, writer, didn't feel immune to the expectations that might be placed upon my work by "professional" poets, by literary "managers."

The thing that I sensed all along, and came to embrace wholeheartedly, was the kind of slipstream I fell into as these poems came to life, magically imprinting themselves into the world, in ways that found their own original form each time. Whether rhyming was the focus or not, whether metering even eventuated, I found a strange and unique manner where the words would flow into their own style of rhyming, or would simply just come into existence in a way that seemed profound enough without trying to hold them to structural preconceptions. As such, I have accepted the message coming through that, yes, they are poems.

In offering this insight, which is all but unnecessary other than to incite the reader into a more mystical mindset, I hope that "automatic writing" or "just show up" parlays into a surrender to the divine, that the veil of stoic expectation of the written word might be lifted up, and a drifting into the mists of the unknown might occur. After all, what is a poem if it is not a mischievous invitation into a softly lit, scented space that threatens to heighten one's senses with a thirst for desire and a dizzying arousal of self?

Arousal is key.

Come, surrender with me.

Catherine Harford, 2022

One Dream Closer to Love

Desert Dreaming

I love your words
Love to follow your feelings
Into the circle
Of creation and existence

Looking for meaning
In the who, what and why
Or is it just
The basting of time

As we body slam
Trance
Dance and redefine
The connection that takes us there

Karma in Advance

Talk to me in sunlight
Kiss me by the moonlight
Wrap me up in big, strong arms
And tell me I'm alright

Save me once a day dear
When craziness comes too near
Help me shoo the demons off
And recall the light that lives here

Be my saving grace
My world enchanting face
The reminder of all in life that's good
My secret, sacred place

I need you here beside me
To quell as they deride me
To sing the song of all along
A loving heart so mighty

A crystal in my hearth
Lover blessed from birth
The one I need to stay with me
As I roam upon this earth

I'll follow you each day
Into dreams of far away
A dance of lights through amethyst nights
An endless drift of play

For life is but a romance
The living proof of one chance
To make it count with every ounce
Of karma in advance

The Quest

Quite a quest
But never protest
When we're on track

You know we're the best
Free of hallmarks
Diluted by bright sparks
The next to none
Of all and some
As we meander down our path

With fun of family fretting
Seems dull and oh so daft
For you are my king sweep
And I clever it out daily

Still I have to pray
For I'm eking it out
In the deepest of sleep

The comfortable tack
For all that I lack
Endeavouring to make it up
Tenfold and overflowing
This gold-rimmed
And smithied cup

We'll take this dirt track
And camp out under the stars
Content with the joy
Of looking back
And celebrating one night more
Together

The Lost Love of Science

The temple of the one-eye
The pyramid of my time
As I've spent and I've roamed
Sought out a new home

Daring to incomplete
As you wash my feet
And I bathe your hair
Into a realm
Of gratitude forceful

Bliss and heart swell
Comfort and loveliness
Blessed contentment
Abandoned resentment

Truth and a shiny cigar
Boxing gloves
And a big scar

The lost science of love
Has bought us this far

Love's Equation

Cast amidst confusion
Loving less intrusion
Tell me how to free this out
To be your best ablution

She doesn't mention it
To passers by
Higher than the highest tree

Glimpsing over valleys
Brand new energy
Bonds grasping
Extending
Photosynthesising

Sunrising patterns
Playing on your cloudy thoughts
Follow me
This is how it's done
Knocking on heaven's door

Hatching your chicks
Laying more bricks
For incredibly strong foundation
Dreaming in an epic location

Shimmer deep our mansion
For lifetime love's equation

Fire Dancing

Talking from your curtained room
Shadowed by a certainty of containment
Disparate in suggestion
Left by cold and deft question

Crisis point?
The nicest joint
Working it so
Making it lo

Fire dancing the wax point
Forgives me unto the night time

Seen it in my dreams
And the firefly seems
To caution this pleasant commotion
You're kneading my love and devotion

Windswept ballistic
Can't feel your dipstick
Wouldn't seem right for the future
But y'are cute ya

Gloved hand
One of the band
When they work it they go so deeply
And I'll respond to you so sweetly
So long as the timing
Is keeping me climbing
Shatter your frugal attrition

My love is your brand new position
Not blind to this flailing condition
Or the love that waits for us there

Bevy of Brunettes

Bevy of brunettes
Brains sparking tall
Casting their driftnets
Gift of one to all

Branches softly breaking
History in the making
Taking the time to redefine
A blustered bosom baking

The cattlement of animal
A web upon the sea
Feast with it in course
Treat it with delicate force

Pristine confinement
Punching out playgroups
Trepidation true
Hand it out to you

And wonder what to do
When she has you calling
You'll fall for it
You'll see

My Jugular

Go for the jugular
Driving in my jaguar
Romance is its own accord
When the timing is right
And neither are bored

Collecting the rhythm and data
No more removal of Sparta
Bleat the discreet
And use your left feet
When the temples will try that much
        harder

Craft me in your whim
Save for me your sin
Jealous retrieval guessed into air
Your jet-like tail speed taking me there

I bask in your sunsets
Sleep in your life-lets
Dream in your bed-wets
Of threshold

The beautiful rainbow of gold
When you make me

Prayer for the Unborn

When I think of you
In my mind's eye
I picture your face
Your tiny embrace

Your qualities
Your personality
The way that you'll unravel me

Your heartbeat strong
And our own love song

The morning hush before you wake
The tears that will make
My own heart break

The pure joy in feeling your skin
A soft bare bum
And a toothless grin

Your hapless determination cries
Ease with mum and dad by your side
The quiet thrill of gurgling laughter
Our very own happily ever after

Our growing seed in the gods' own care
So close to our thoughts
And hearts to bare

And if angels could hear how very much
Reach for you with a whispered touch
Protect you, keep you safe from harm
Until we can feel you in our arms

Kind Folk

The kindliest of folk
Would share naught but a joke
For in a while
When you find that you smile
You'll feel nothing but stoked

Because their hearts are true

Everflow

    Cradling my withering heart
    Beggaring hope with each new start
    That echoes over ranges
    The feeling oh so strange

    Looking for kicks
    Long after closing time
    Tasting resonance
    Of something decadent
    That lingered
    Along the wire

    Burning away
    The bushfire
    Happy tornadoes
    Making their way
    Through dreamtimes

    Come dance with me
    Get crazy
    As the night draws on

    As stars dazzle with each song
    Rhythm and heat
    Shuffle to the drumbeat
    Burning up the radio

    The heat of your everflow

Seven Towers

Seven flowers
Lining the paths
To seven towers

Just For You

Girl I gotta give in
Cause you're drivin' me wild
Just believe in me woman
I'll be your child

My defences are down
Nothin' else I can do
Say you'll stay one more night
You know I'll be true

All I'm askin' for
Is a piece of your time
My heartbeat is raw
I want you as all mine

When I look in your eyes
It's all shiny and new
Look at me here babe
It's all just for you

Reverie

The drums are reaching fever pitch
And the trouble starts
My heart is kicking in
Melody sinking in
Right through me

I can't explain
This rhythmic reverie
Set upon
From the earliest sense
Of you and me

We collide
We blend
We meld into one another
And once more
I make you my lover
As ancient scriptures willed

Spilling all over you
A sense of you
Of dreams coming true
And the best we could ever do

Giving of each other
Freely enjoying
The sister and brother
The purest versus the annoying
But what else can we do?

In the long run
There's only the finest sense
Of me and you

As long as the cat milks the cream
And in the privacy of our own worlds
You generate my sensual scream
I guess we'll burn
For one another

And the bizarre face of love
Will illuminate all else
That we inadvertently smother
Death nells washed away

Lovers in their private play
Made fresh and new
Ready to face
Any kind of brand new day

And the sounds of
Our musical interference
Will ultimately be
The making of
A brand new reverie

Stay

As long as I know you
It can rain all year round
The trains can run late
The trees can stay bare
Dogs can cry all night
People don't have to smile
The clock can keep ticking
You can be with her
And my bed can stay empty

As long as I know you

Lovers

Walk with me in my life
Share a space with me by my side
Let us guide one another
And share a laugh and some love
Along the way

Spirits of a Kind

The kindred find us dreaming
On the outskirts of town
Calling upon all manner of pastimes
To see us through

The blossoming of this wild thing
This escapism
This Cote d'Azur
Of pristine imagination

Try rambling across my coastline
Get lost with me
Sample the wilderness
That sets me free

As I journey into dimensions
That fly so far
From the mundane
From the backward nature of normal

I formally invite you
To taste of the night time
To enjoy the starlight
That shines when you don't notice

Dance with me
Beyond the backyard
Fly with me
Along windswept oceans

Set fire to sunsets
That blaze brighter than you care
Imagine you're running
Faster than you've ever dared

We're supermen
We're Robin Hood
And his merry men
Thieving the good stuff to keep

Quick! Take it all!
May as well
The other have fallen asleep!

So many riches for the taking
Let them forsake it
If all they want are things
Daydreams awaken
Receive your soul to sing

Look out over yonder
Beyond the white and blue
Doorways, portals, dimensions
Beckoning, summoning you

Dance, come and dance free spirit
Alight on form so fair
And I shall seek the wonderment of all
With you, somewhere out there

The Great Mother

I gaze out at the view
In wonder and awe
Feeling the sense of accomplishment
Rushing over me
Like a wave
In my own beautiful ocean

My own personal slice
Of the Pacific
Granted to me in this moment
That came to me in dreams
From so long ago

And now I know
How much she loves me
As I breathe her in
And she breathes me out

We blend as one
She takes me into
Her bushy bosom
And I fold beneath
Her warmth and care

Feeling the truth of my purpose
And how much she needs me here

A Poem for Frank and Kel

Home is where the heart is
And my heart is in this place
Summoning so many feelings
When I gaze upon your face

The warmth and care and comfort
That we hold deep in our souls
A space to grow and love and change
Till we're grey and we are old

Our lives were so connected
It was written in the stars
That should we stall and sometimes fall
Our journey takes us far

So hold my hand as we stand
In the space that's all our own
For in your eyes I recognise
The place that we call home

Angel Girl

Beyond life and death
A love so vast
There are no boundaries
Only time and space
To make it your place

You'll be home
And when they ask where
You won't say

Only you, girl
Will know the way there

I'll wait
And I'll greet you
Like you never left
Without you
We're nowhere

Aiming for perfection
Won't reach you a star

You know who you are
C'mon girl, dance, sing
I'll bring you the fruits
Of your love

Breathe easy, girl
Heaven's waiting
For you

Wild Australia

Where will I find her?
The silver moon
I hear them calling
The sun and the moon

I cannot see them
Locked here in my room
I long to find them
The sun and the moon

Where is my brother?
Dancing in the fire
Where is my brother?
Dancing higher and higher

Where is my sister?
Where desire is true
Wild Australia
I will come for you

The Fondu of Time

Gestation periods spent
Acclimatising with you
Suspended in space
Heartbeats reminded
And fractions in time

Natal tracts

Steal from me
The plagiarism of our love
Repeat it to me
Until I know it off by heart

Grummed respect
Destiny
A fondu of time
Spent with you

Tethered

    Strips of love
    Tether me here
    Beyond my comprehension

    Adhesion
    Too strong to mention

The Finke

Fresh out of advice
Listening to the blues
And remembering old times
Old rhymes

Places that came and went
Time spent in a heartbeat
Palm trees that swayed
Songs that played
Next to open campfires
Under southern skies
Stars shining brightly
And a soft moon lingering

Dancing in the sand
Of the riverbed
Ancient songlines
Beneath our sandy feet
Resonating through the ages

To touch our souls
And connect us
To a time and a place
That we'll recall
For all our days

A crazy haze of friendship
Of Aboriginal magic
Of freedom

The Boy

The boy is pale and willing

His hand is driving
The future of tokens
And his wish
Is to be with her

To tell her that
She's made just right
And give her
What he can

He's wrapping her up
In comfortable thoughts
Trusting that
The satisfaction to come
Is second to none

Fun times
And fresh giggles
Leave an aerated tone

Confidence weens him
From the teat
Of inexperience

Dream Big

Meet me at the top of the mountain
I'll make it there, one day soon
Skipping over rocks and branches
Planting myself
With each arduous footstep

Up and up, one after another
I will myself on
Past the pain
The sweet agony of resistance
A body out of form
That wants to feel free again
To feel alive

I strive forward
With heaving breath
As I climb on
Towards that pinnacle
That place I have dreamed of
For so long

Where my needs are met
My dreams come true
And you heal me
Once and for all

Sealing me into a self
That knows and does on cue
Without stalling

Without faltering
Without fear of falling
From up so high

I see it
The sky
So close I could touch it

Nearer to heaven
Than I've ever come
So far

One Step Forward, Two Steps Back

The Emotional Void

When I feel your hand
According to my breast
And the rest
Is some sort of mind play

Where I stay and persuade
Jade and renegade
Defend my position
Adjust to the transition
Of life to wife

Will you commit
To the gift that sits
Somewhere from you to me
The somewhere in between

Requesting night time
Lover's flight
Believing the call
Or pressuring the fall

It's nothing new
Just seems so little else
For me to do

Other than satisfy you

The Fundamental Crusade

Breaking headlines
Front page news
An article from our best
Journalist extraordinaire

Real life thou will attest
Summation of the facts
No bias there to see
Genuflect so humbling
She cares for you and me

Minds will now wander
And take it all on board
Seeds of doubt planted fine and firm
She shoots and then she scores

And as the daily news unfolds
Third page, not rating mention
Till stumbled acts outland afoot
Aha! She's right!
Come take a look!

Grinning, smiling
Harvesting thoughts
Hmm, yes, I see
I totally agree

Opinions mounted
Vain ablaut
Dreamlike entelechy

Weapons amounted
Entente cordiale
She's made her mark
She'll make her move

Enshrouded battlement
Subliminal bullets
Dusting off the records
All focused on you

Until you're cornered
Covered
Cowering
In her fundamental crusade

Between the milking and the maid
How else can you be saved?

Old Sydney Town

The lantern swinging
Lighting my path
Guiding my way
Along cobblestone streets
The distant, muffled clip-clop
Of horses' sturdy feet

The fog so thick and dense
Blocking out the night
The moon and the stars
Bring a pearly, iridescent light

Weaving through back alleys
Up smartly, down promptly
And nary a lamp
Left lit at such a time

Tucked into bed
The city sleeps
Barring mournful horns
Of boats upon the harbour

Still I hear the whisper
Of water lapping at land-lips
Of possums scampering
Looking for food
And the far-off cackles
Of prostitutes at work
Echoing so clearly
Through this town

This land of much intrusion
This outpost that meets
The ends of the earth
As the last untouched, great continent
Is overrun

The Saming

Rue the day
You samed me
I am not like that
But are you?

Making peace with intention
And finding the message with all
So I can hurry up
And get the hell out of here

Into another room
With double-glazed glass
Where I can still be near
To this place
That I'm meant to be

Where you can still see me
But can't get to me
No longer to be hurt
By your positivity

Boondocks of irruption
The best of your intention
Making your way through life
With naught but a belief
In some other way

Mother?
Please
Spare me the fray

What am I Holding Onto?

Dominated and breathing
The art of receiving
The clairvoyant act
Of most deft believing

Swear it threefold
Can you unsheathe?

If the tree fathom be bold
Then stand strong
Along with me

How can you hold
Onto nothing
So tightly?

Love and Devotion

Offer me this ring
In a ritual
Of love and devotion
Slices of my life
Are chunks
Adorned by you

My sword
Stinging in its belt
Determined to stick you
Out of this race
To get away and find peace
A place of freedom
To see it all undone

Second to none
You frighten me more
Than any man before

Believing in partisan
You seem closer than me
Yet I thought it was I
Who was the devoted one?

But I stumble betwixt my run
Longing out
The day I'm done
As you gaily revive
Nothing bad to come

Aah, this is madness!
I'm tormented by your gladness!
When you trickle-feed your existence
So consistently

Left to ponder
My own asunder
Duped by the dowdiness
Or lack of loveliness

Nothing like a tongue kiss
To fire and fuel my passion

The Frenemy

The partial proliferation
Of this damning contract
Our stoic, yet subconscious agreement
Determining how we act

Our spectre of social graces
Calamity of too many faces
Donning our feelings in moments
Awareness of each one's atonements
Redressing overwhelming distaste
For one cannot afford to lose face

In light of differing opinion
The arrogance of one's own dominion
Sequestrate serpentine nature
The vassal of fate that's been wagered

Comically spoken in trips
Beliefs and true passions
Eroding the fashions
And the words that come past your lips

Lose the apparence
Pig-swill and snipe fish per Havants'
We exchange the best that we muster
Indulging our idolum fluster

Will our minds ever let us be friends?
We'll just have to see at the end

Shoulders to Cry On

Shoulders to cry on
Made of iron
Hold such little comfort

As I seek softness
Find hardness
Coldness
And a steely indifference

Oh, for a tender breast
A soft bosom
To weigh myself on
To nestle into
And finally find reprieve

Oh, this lonely life
This disconsolate
Confusing repertoire
Of lofty emotions
That never bother
To float to earth
For long enough
To ever really
Feel anything

If only I
Could hide in a bubble too
Shelter in a cocoon
And all too soon
Find the wings
That would help me
Fly far away from here

From the scathing appraisal
Of my heartfelt tears

The Fool

I am

I am a fool
I am the child
I'm the infantile
The most worthless cog
In the microcosm

I am useless

I am the inane representation
Of the absence of greatness
The empty spaceness
Of a life that's amounted
To nothing
The amassing of little
That would do
To amaze the masses

To impress the passers by
Of my life
With the speed
The zip
Of keeping up

The in-step
The hot-shoe-shuffle
Of the most luxurious
Human fluffle

The ferfluffle
Snuggling into
The being of a smashing lifetime
Overflowing with good times
And expensive wines
Dripping in gold
And free-pass lifelines

An endless bounty
Of moonlit night times
Romantic highs
And the abundant lust of supplies
Of supple thighs on tap

A fool with no grand reward
For mastering the race
For devouring space and resources
That could be shared by many
But are hoarded by the few

The winners, the succeeders
Who are paid their due

I am a fool
A fool who berates and negates
The notion of her very existence
As to why I am brimming over
With the very resistance
That keeps me from
Being rewarded
In the same fashion

Taking my place on the podium
Of human Olympic endeavours
The master of my pleasures
And a reverie
Of creative output

An offshoot
Of the artistic industries
That can actually afford
To monopolise a space
In the fabric of
The cultural dream machine
For me

Where only one or two
Can slip through
At any given time

Here's one!
Palatable
Marketable
A fool for the rules
And the right thing to do
Too easy

I am a fool
For trying too hard
For not trying enough
For being a pushover
For talking too rough

I am a fool for kindness
I'm a sitting duck
Sitting in a stupor
Whilst getting royally fucked

Aware of the shittiness
Lost in disbelief
Weathered by innumerable storms
Drowning in my grief

Mute to horrible behaviours
Dumb to not speak them aloud
Trapped by this terminal kindness
That forbids me to be too proud

Humiliated by the offing
How quickly they take off my head!
And laugh, how they laugh at me so!
How they wish me all but dead

They trample my good nature
They feed on my broken brow
For I am a fool, I see it clearly
How they love to now the brown cow

I am a fool, in turns, it's true
And in turns, the magician comes
Each foolish time, I take it in
I wait . . . and in time
Wisdom comes

I see through the façades
Through yours, and through mine
I see it with compassion
Through the shattered shards of time

I see through the pain and heartache
I see obliteration and more
I see beyond the unforgivable
And I see what redemption is for

I learn from all your foibles
From your cunning, greed and lust
I see through to your conditioning
That to succeed is an absolute must

You become the dog, eating the dog
You lift up the rulebook, you declare
You scatter your beliefs and your systems
Showering all that will come back to you
        so fair

You demand the respect of your wishes
As you piss on others at will
And as long as the rules are fairly stated
It's as good to do as you feel

If your feeling is lust, then you take it
You plunder all to be found
If your feeling is treasure, you make it
And stand your footing aground

Pity the fool who fights me
Pity them and the day
And you armour yourself to do battle
To defend yours and your lot this day

A fool to sit by and allow it
A fool not to get up and fight?
But spirituality is not sorcery
And magic will always be right

The peasant who has supped at your table
The receipt of generosity absurd
The pawn in your cat and mouse game
The poor little wounded bird

I have been screamed at and shouted
    down in my own home
Humiliated as I dined at my own table
Demonstratised and demonised
Diminished into little more than a fable

I have sat undefended aplenty
Whilst abused and neglected in turn
Bore witness to flashed tits and bare
    fannies
As the they were thrust in the face of my
    man

I have reeled and I have sat quietly
    outraged
Wounded and seething and sore
I have crawled up into balls and have cried
Yet I have lived a hundred lifetimes or
    more

I have cursed the architect of my nature
For journeying me so long through
    wounded pride
Forever a fool to my good graces
Forever a fool to my goddesses, gods and
    guides

Forever a fool to the whisper of Pan
To Eros, unsheathed and unshod
Forever a fool for the Galactic Mind
The bidding of the one and greatest God

The Lonely Witch

Oh! For the girl of 23!
How destitute was she?
How lonely and alone
In her witchy ways

Bewitched by nature
And the heady bounty
Of her beauty

A wonder like no other she could name

The Love We Share

We nest in the love we share
Searching for the life
That grows there
Right? Don't we?

Yet tonight, I toss and turn
On my bed of board
Screaming and crying
For the words we don't speak

You know, in your dreams
As I do
That we're scared
We're just trying to find our way

Relief will come
With the eagle's flight
Though for now I bid you
Farewell, and goodnight

Crush the Patriarchy

    I am not ready to believe
    Not ready to receive the goodness
    The future brings

    He's watching me
    Judging me

    His green eyes burn
    Into the back of my neck
    And he wills no more
    Can it be done

    How do I shun
    This black-hearted scoundrel?
    Where does he end
    So I can begin?

    How do I chase him
    From my door?
    Say no more
    Will you steal my light

    Just one more night

    I'm not that strong
    It must be wrong
    Have me break confidence
    Why not?

    I'm not ready to believe

Jealous Tongues

Jealous tongues wagging
Such very nasty talk
Makes me balk at the notion
Of how sweet
How complete
How esculent to the rest of the world
You especial kind of girls

Emotion cheap to fritter
Is tasting rather bitter
Escalade abandoned castle
Auger your definitive parcel

Cresting parataxis
Wishing me to hell
When I admit it to you now
We don't see eye to eye

How could we?
You'll never see me fly

Parlance of romantic vision
Held to by this indecision
Paid it in your chances
When all you do is lance

Cutting down the life
Boredom wields its strife
Simple itinerate turn on
To have me in your nest
Ascus of my best

Insane dualogue
Comes down to you and me

Ballyhoo suppression
Keep for you your prize
But to tell so many lies
May not be so wise

The Unholy Nuisance

You can't!
I'm almost there!
Resign your interest
In a child so fair

She's not yours
Not really

She might resemble you in ways
But her likeness is that of a god
Or so she's been told
And she's bold enough to believe

So leave, leave her be
You're not welcome here
Leave her be

Let her do what she has to
She doesn't need your interference
You unholy nuisance
You must leave

My door is closing

The Wall

When the hope starts to fade
I find every reason
To stop believing

The things I've seen
The places I've been
Subside a stretch

As the bricks slot into place
To build the wall
That I'll knock down
Time and again

I falter under
Its drastic weight
My sturdy pace
Grinds to a halt

I stand here in ruins
Uncertain
Which way to turn

Craving peace in my solitude
And the courage to have faith
In that
Which is shown to me

Red and Blue

Creep along the corridors of your mind
Peek behind the curtains, red and blue
Cast your eyes over the memories there
Try and grasp the real you

Deceit, misfortune, trivial pursuit
Depths never dived into
Shallows murky from eternities of wading
A pierced shell you crawled out from
To distance yourself from the hurting

What is it you want?
Expect this will pay off?
As the child wails and kicks and screams
Blinding the hole in her shadow land
With so many current dreams

To try and live
To try and fight
A body war torn and ravaged by hunger
Spoiled by luxuries
Too numerous to hold up
In the broken light of day

The real me?
I don't know what to say

The Judge

Trying hard
To understand
The pain in my heart
The ache in my bones
The state of my being

Seeing as
Here in my hands
Blends a fine mixture
Of time
And planetary rotation

Your philistinic placation
Sits uneasily with me

Can't you see
When I avert my eyes
Divert my movement
Your attunement
To a place that's all your own

I am nothing more
Than a visionary illusion
Just to mend your confusion
Of that which you thought
I truly was

Faith

Frightened decibels are learning
To conquer the passages of time
Hanging and framing the realities
That treatise truths
Of current power

Telling yourself
There's no bad karma
While holding on
To flatulent dreams

Solemnities
Beliefs
And situations
That far outdate themselves

Mask pasts to update checklists
And don't believe for a second

Wailing tisms
Fruit positions
And Christian faith
Is holding you dear

Wait near the design of conflict
We'll call you when you're ready

Laced in salutation
Stems no further
Than blossomed head

Gallipolise me
The war is over there
Near that country

Try to be neutral in all holdings
Hope for the best

Are You the One?

The level of your sincerity
Is tearing at the heart of me
Peeling away layers of skin
Only to reveal
A fresh cocoon
To gum up this divide

And far too soon
I'm sunken deep
Nuisance chatter
Away to keep
Yet hoping for a breakthrough

My butterfly body beating
A restless spirit seeking
Tasting the juice
This lover sent

You wish me as Houdini
We both try hard to free me
Longing to dance in rhythms
Patterned by heart explosions

As night time falls
And moonlight calls
Desire will trip discretely

A new adventure
With every touch

Your lips brush over my body
Inflaming sensation
The passionate persuasion
Is criminal not to feel

As destiny confronts me
And demands that it be real

Wander and Fade

Deviant knickers
Perilous flickers
Of hot flames
You seem so familiar
With these particular games

I try to reach you
With our common themes
Carelessly treading
On broken dreams
And a strong sense
Of always trying

Let's face it
The rites of this phase
Are dying

And I'd be lying
If I said
I miss them much

A stone's throw away
Your dormant touch
When my heart's arrest
Still attests
To the best I've known

But my new lover's so little
And every bit of her
Reminds me of home

So that my mind
Continues to whittle
Our connection away to naught

And for all the years we fought
To remain abreast
Of the damning tests
That all lovers face

I wander and fade
Amidst your embrace

Icy, Soulless Day

Desperately driving
Through several forms
Hoping to tap into
The standard norms
Sunken, wet and scared
She barely performs
On an icy, soulless day

Hoping the marvel she makes
Will transpire
A happiness held
Together with wire
That somehow will serve
To quench this desire
On an icy, soulless day

Time travel, mineral love
Unnerving chilled pleas
A quivering notion
A lifelong disease
As pirates come forth
And plunder her seas
On an icy, soulless day

I'll wait for that
Which might possibly save me
For defeat is a word
That makes me uneasy
Till then will the truth
Ever actually please me?
Just an icy, soulless day

Katherine

Katherine was a woman
Who didn't know when
To call in
Her lucky strike
And throw her cards in

Like a dog with a bone
She held on

The Survivors

Two ghosts
Rolling around the same space
Haunting each other
With a bleak reality

Memories
Times lost
The past
Catching up too fast

With a notion
Of here and now
Empty time and space
Empty movement

Making room
For an ocean
That crashes over you
Like a tidal wave

But we don't drown
You and I

We survive

Time is Up

I sat down
Under a tree
With my heart
In my hands

I sat it down next to me
Wet with sickening, bittersweet emotion
You have five minutes to dry it out
They seemed to say
On such a sunny day

Tinder box brain
Fire brewing
Trying to stem the flames of forbearing
Wearing bitter jitters on my sleeve
For all the world to see

Doesn't look that cool after all
It never does
My insecurity

Hmm, yet somehow at the moment
It tells the truth of me
Or does it?

Rubbing wrong ways
Time is ticking
Checking that stickiness
Of certain thoughts

Like glue
Stuck to you
This bitter emery board
Endlessly scratching
At such a soft surface

Time is up, they say
Pick up your heart
You can go now

One Night Closer to Death

Present Tense

All these minutes that master me
All this recollection that devours me
All of the memories that I'm bound to see
Count for something that amounts to me

It's how I choose to spend my time
It's the way that makes me feel sublime
It's destiny at its worst crime
If it weren't for needing to feel it's mine

I'm longing to own it
I'm needing to borrow
The measure of forgiveness
And the heartlessness of sorrow

If I wanted you here
I'd howl at the moon
And wager you'd come
None too soon

Spinning in circles
Divine countenance
The truth, come what may
With all present tense

I choose to believe
That's all that makes sense

Winter Blues

I am
Something and nothing
Everything and all
A failure of conviction
And possibilities beyond measure

A life span of dried leaves
Scrunching of faces
Put through the paces
When the chill sets in my bones

I whine and whimper
Sympathising the season
Rendering every reason
A hardship of notedness
But only if you notice

Dare to make comment
Of another well spent hour
Awaiting the sun and bloom'ed flower

Harking toward rich pelts
Maybe when the ice melts
I'll thaw out once more

Come back to life
Sharpen the knife
And carve it all anew

When Spring finally comes
Knocking on my door

Terra Karma

Tanami to Rabbit Flat
Can't get there
And how to get back
Desperate in our search for
The black heart
Of the country

Eking out the destiny
Of truth in our rebellion
The white hand of fear
Is gripping at my breast

With all your scruples
Put to test
Because you've never loved
In the way that they've loved

Never seen
The way they've dreamed

Your white honkey's arse
Fattened with cream
And still your demand
Is for more

The much more yet
And Mother Nature
Knows the score

Tears in My Soup

There are tears in my soup
As the heavens open up
And mourn my solemn hour

Alone, once more

Reminded of my failures
As I have borne
The failures of others

I've tried, no one can say I haven't
A devil-may-care savant
Whose powers have only grown
Even this far from home

With the nurture
And the torture
Of so much good fortune
Of fae in their element

They're heaven-sent
I know they are

As I've battled and cried
Loved and lied
About how much it's cost
To love so and still feel lost

Not apart
But not a part of
Clipped wings for a caged peace dove
Reminiscing celestial love

The powerful magic that came and went

And just when I thought
My holy grail was close
That after all
There might be some repose

I see the white rabbit
Calling me on
For my time here
Is nearly done

And if that which I reach for
Dissipates
It'll be a goal
Which will just have to wait

Any love we share
Will just have to keep
And sleeping dogs
Will finally be left to sleep

Samsara Now

Dress me up
In your likeness
I want to feel the rhythms
And persuasions

A thousand faces
From a thousand nations
Relative to form
And dialect

Detecting
The nocturnal convenance
Of each tribe

The bourgeois cleverness
Staid responses
Ensconced in compassion

Grandiose fashion
Educated by
The powers that be
Relative to nothing
But monotone filagree

Little would we know
That the stone was set to throw
And had we tested bored
We'd have rested further accord

For something should be done
Under familial sun
Yet it's difficult to act
When truth leaves you numb

After all we all are many
As primary as it hallows
And should the gods prove more
We'll reach within their shallows

For action is unjust
And rhetoric is a must
For a film was all it was
So why the sudden mistrust?

Paradise Lost

Here I lay
Prisoner to my own
Tropical paradise
All that should
Feel so nice
Succumbing to
My favourite vice

Strings suspended
In the air
Not sure anyone
Even cares

Testing flares
Of lucid dreams
With all who
Wonder and seem
To devote themselves
To what it's like

I hide beneath the moonlight
I test the bounds of what's right
For here I crave a fixture true
A constant sense of what is you

I flipped the switches
I pulled the triggers
I gave it all
For ecstatic figures

My red shoes are in flight
Looks like they're white tonight
Baby this is all it takes
Yet still my heart aches

If I had the courage
To taste your sting
The solemn sense
To let you in
I'm aware that
We'd stand to remain

But I feel the grass
Beneath my feet
And the sun
Beating down on me
And the hum of cicadas
Resonates

A meditation
An Australian solution
Paradise found
And lost

Tremulous Truths

Moments of time
Barely touch
Barely graze
When suddenly
You faze me out

Do I linger on your skin?
Did I ever even begin
To touch the place
You might call home?

Were we ever really alone?
As ghosts wrestle
To lay claim
To all our time

Were we ever going to find
A long forgotten land?
A dream to escape in
A face to face rhyme

As I recall
Longing in the looks
You gave to me
Maybe just a phase

A dreamlike trace
Of sensual exposure
Giving it to me
Over and over

But apparently it's nothing
In the scheme of things
As rectitude seeks
Understanding of flings

We were barely attuned
To the stars
To the moon
At least according to you

Yet for me
It felt true

As I stand in ruins
Heartbreak abounding
I'm left with the whisper
Of love resounding

So call me a fraud
If that's what you need
Paint it as devastation
Deny the primal feed

But know as much
Feel my score
You win no matter what
As I recover burnt and raw

For I'm burned alive by your love
I will be forever more
And the feelings left to explore
Could tear down a thousand doors

As you cast me aside for the last time
I hope you live to be sure

I Was Meant for Bigger Things

I focused on the circle
In my mind's eye
Gnawing at the edges
The infinite downward spiral
That never goes viral

Trying to think up something
So fundamentally clever
That the nature of my being
My exasperating existence
Would be so much better

The fervour of my creative block
The infinitesimal desire for more
Or at least a star-shaped niche
Associated with my name

Believing deep down
I was meant for so much more
For the grandest of entrances
Through the wide and ornate door

The open wound of my soul
The absence of self
The spectacular reminder of failure
Of the dimensional pulse
Of my fading heartbeat
That once resounded
So strongly

Afterlife

The shadows creak
Yawn and stretch
Testing distance of those
No longer with us

Lights flicker
Play tricks on you
Making believe
You're not alone

Wanting to feel
That it could be real
That the essence now gone
Could live on

But you chide and chastise
Blaspheme and realise
That it can never be
Nothing left to see

So what is that whisper
In your ear?
What is that calling
You feel
But can't hear?

Is it just me?
Am I wishful thinking?
Or will it one day sink in
The truth of life's palladium
An essence that is winking
Flickering, sparkling
Dancing before
Your very eyes

Another dimension
In mute disguise
Just a test of aptitude
To feel the real thing

The way of it all
Beyond the sense
Beyond the call
In space divine
And spinning

Vibrating
Ambling
Heavenly and rambling
Through that which
We believe
Is for sure

When you approach
That other zone door

Try to open your mind
And trust what you find
As that which lives
Forever more

For Nan

DNA
Molecules
Cells
Time

A passage
A presence that passes through
A connection to memory
A flowing of energy

First with light and love
Fluidity
An echo chamber of voices
That will become your whole world

Your existence
Each passing day
Day after day after day
So mundane
So profound

And little by little
Your story grows
Your world expands
Your love multiplies

Suddenly a slipstream
So many years have passed
An army of offspring
Are dancing in your wake

Worlds are colliding
Feelings rampage
A perfect mess of hearts and minds
The symphony of your life

And somewhere down on Prince St
Queen Elsie sits and waits
Perched on her throne of bird calls and
                flowers
And history of this place

The shining light of your face
The dust and musty scents
The eternally familiar embrace
Of our connection to you

Time breaks
Time has broken
I've woken up
To a new reality

One that seems empty
Where you're not here for me
Even though
I can sense that you are

You didn't go far

But what I wouldn't give
For one more cup of tea
One more trip to the miner's cottage
With you waiting by the gate

Waiting with a joke
Or a warning
Or a complaint
That only a nanna can give

Oh what I wouldn't give
For one more kiss goodbye
If only in my dreams, Nan
One last cuddle goodbye

Sundancer

    Much sufferance or desire
    Could lend me my mind
    If it were sensible to be
    Anyone but me

    Alas, merely a girl
    Of twisted fate

    A woman
    Of pure thought
    Impure thoughts

    Divinity ought
    To see her through
    These lonely nights

    When to see
    Her glowing face
    Her aching heart
    Her arching back

    Sundancing
    Under the heat
    Of his touch

I bid you, come
Seek me out
Mind my spirit
As I heed your soul

How well will we know?
Dare I ask the question
When I cannot let it be

"True enough", she says
"I confess it all to thee"

I am this and more
And less by the light of this candle
Forgiveness?
Redemption?

A thick, warm hand
In the small of her back
Let her know she's alive

Fortuna

Fortuna abide by me
Reside with me
In the solemn hour

Recall the truth
Of every flower
That has lived and died

Inside and beyond
The essence of those
That still live on

Fly on, dear ones
Far and wide and long

Fly on
Fly on

The Emptiness

All the words I used last night
They do me no service
They serve me no interest
Leaving gaps of space
That long to be filled

Fulfilled

That's a word I didn't use last night

Seven Year Itch

What is this moment?
Loving you to death
The myth of sincere benevolence
Struck by hardcore evidence

Spell bound by half time
My seven year itch
And its providence

The Incessant Sin

Your dismay
Trembled the legend
That was being made
Left wondering how
Your holiday ear
Metronome of flat line cheer
Yet still you claim the mettle

Happy, accomplished
And distaste is wept for howling
If only phoenetically
She'd spelled it out to thee

Could've sympathised
Could've roamed
Could've honed in
Could've clouded this
Incessant sin

But you never bothered to ask
So you'll never really know
Never really grasp

Balance Restored

A fairly local concept
The object of meaning
The regret
The distribution of geography
It's biased and tinged with lethargy

The willingness to move
The desire to be
Somewhere else
Beyond what
You think you see

The fulfillment of a dream
The fantasy of what may seem
The method that makes the cream
The absurd Australian slipstream

Come along, sense the power
Vibrations abound in night time hours
Heavily invested in crucified towers
Blissful repose of self-indulgent gowers

Willing the universal forces
To right things

That Which You Bring to the Party

Only with one life to live
Only one more sin to forgive
Driven by the force of need
Hungry, greedy for the good life

The chance to have it all
And command more

My willingness to make it come
Shouldn't enter into the argument
Of whether or not I deserve it

Serving you up
With my trump card

Overseeing
Overdoing
Overruling
All that you bring to the party

Running Out of Time

Clocks are ticking everywhere
Driving me to despair

Times that tickle
Behind my knees

How quickly I fall
I beg and plead

To feel the presence of your grace
Once more

There's More to Come

    Holding up mirrors
    Reflection
    Introspection
    And a damning regret
    Of time wasted
    Etched like rivers
    Coursing across
    The face of me
    Across the space
    In this world
    That's me

    Staring across an ocean
    Fingering a design
    In the sands of time
    A picture of something
    I might have been
    The dream inside
    I haven't seen for a while

    Something holds me here
    A pattern
    A behaviour
    A maelstrom of decisions
    A battlement of collisions
    That tear at me
    And rip me apart

As old as I may be
I don't know where to start

I built these castles in the sand
But the tide washed over them
And swept them away
My bravery, my defences are gone
My ego, my pride is wounded

I'm grounded, rooted to the spot
As waves rush toward me
And threaten to drown
Put an end to my misery

"Who are you?" I cry to skies above
"What do you want from me?
Have you no pity?
Can't you see?
I'm all come undone!
This is the most wretched I'll be!"

I want to die
I don't know why
But the pain is too much
And I can't touch anything
That stays

All the love
The hope
Seems to go away

I lost the game of life
I'm overwhelmed with strife
And I long to finally be free
From all the hurt inside

And just when I think
I can't take anymore
There's a sense
A faint glimmer of something

A calling
A belonging
An awareness
Deep inside

This isn't the end of the ride

The Grass is Greener

The crippling reality
Of a life spent
In a dark space
Hating the reality
Of what you know
But can't seem
To escape from

Try this, they say
To escape the fray
Pray and dream
Create a new scene

And they're right, you know
Until the same old
Creeps back in
And you're filled
With disrepair

If only I
Could make my way
Over there

The grass looks greener
And I've seen bright sheets
Of dazzling, colourful suggestion
The truth of images
That can't lie

And you seem so young
So vibrant
So perfect

Touching on
The infinite space
Of worldly approval

Removing the lines of time
And the face replaces
Awkward spaces
With its dazzling smile

But after a while
You feel compelled
To tell the truth

That somewhere deep
In your soul
You keep a box
Tied up
With a beautiful bow
Stashing memories
With the hope
That one day
You'll know

That all your time spent
Under traceable government
Of universal will
Was worth it

That each day
Each hour
Each minute
Was perfect

Only you cling to your box
And you feel outfoxed
By the cunning
Of extreme division

That somehow you lost
And you live with the ghost
Of an untimely
Lack of provision

That when they made you
They made you poor
They made you question
Everything and all it's for

And in doing so
They left you sore
Sore and raw
With the whipping of heartbeats

Of lost souls
And empty streets
No one
To come running
To save you

No one to care
No one to share
No one to dance
To your tune

You're terrified
You're hurt
You're sick to death of poverty
And the severe lack of harmony
That's afflicted on you daily

But even as you sit
Crying, wailing
Remember
It's you

It's always been you
The luck you have
You were able to choose

Skewed vision aside
You chose this crazy ride
It was all you

And no amount of basking
In pretty impermanence
Your virtual presence
Can cast that aside

You are the master
The creator of your dream
It's always been you
In the heart of the slipstream

You show them
What it really means
Because you helped design
This reality

Set Me Free

    The years of neglect
    Have taken their toll
    You wonder that I rock
    When you try to roll

    Don't flay my flight
    When you try to capture me
    When you long kept me bound
    But never set me free

The Grieving

My baby's are rotting in their new grave
Talented and dead
Vibrant now they're gone
Spinning around in their new form

The feast was in the making
And now that I think about it
They were there for the taking

But their essence is scattered
All over my front porch
And I have no one now
To come home to

I'm braving this
But I was braver before
When I had you both resting in my sights
With your soft downy touch
And comical delights

Do I just think myself lucky?
Or cry my eyes out
Suddenly wanting to hold you
More than ever

And if loneliness creeps in
Where your warmth used to calm me
Will I still feel you?
Will you stay with me?
Will I chance upon a sparkle
Whenever I recall

The design of your love
In life
Together

Be
Be
All around me

And up above us
As owls hoot satiation by night time
The chapter we've shared
Begins to close

The Twilight of Loneliness

Bleeding on the outside
Has a notorious way
Of judging you into corners
If the moment is a fray

And what of laughing lovers
Deciding what to wear?
Believing that two syllables
Will cover them to stare

Cause in the limelight offers
Party lapses make a frown
But tell as much to carers
Will only bring them down

So if the light is falling
Judge not from you to me
Till nature has us calling
'Bout then no cancer scree

For loneliness is twilight
And fiskes are trenched to ground
Listen to winds roaring
Friends soon will be around

The Witch from Oz

There was a young girl from Australia
Whose wizardry just couldn't ail 'er

She tried and she tried
Then she cried and she cried
When all those around seemed to fail 'er

Sheep

Land on my cushion bot
The free reign
Of ecclesiastic learning

Warning apparel
And a darkened hand lends
Friends and cigarettes

Social mends
Behaving in fashions
Lasting the outlasted moment
Of rhymes

Mirth and no feeling
Currency of stealing
As the culture sways

You stay where you are
Before you comes
Agnostic likening

Frightened we may be herd
But we bleat all the same

The Void

Crossing the timelines
Of forgiveness

What once was
And now is
See if you can pick
The difference

Your absence
Cold heart deliverance
Telling me I'm stupid
And unwelcome

Yet the void here
Is like the Grand Canyon
And I never was
Much of an engineer

So how do you propose
We build this bridge?

Maybe a super-powered rocket blaster
Can bring me to your side
But I fear concurrent battalion
My early dying bride

Never mind
We'll make amends
Maybe
One day

One Prayer Closer to Awake

The Lightest Prayer

The whispered words
Of faery tales
Dance upon my thoughts

And through the ache of my tears
I determine to resurrect
The magic bestowed
With every touch

A symphony of lines
Come rushing in
To heal a wounded heart

And the rain pours down

Hidden Colour City

Blocking the deception
Of fragmentary human exception
To expansion
And the freak waves
Of free flowing
Violent misconception

The precept is wary
Wayward
And frightening

Scary blaring
Human horror
Scarring one's youth
Into corners

Heaven
Merely a device
Of healing

And reeling in
The unwanted pugnacity
Of a mindful condition

Fruiting water shoots
And friendly spiels
The freeze frame condition
Of a star born nexus

Earthbound in trying
And developmental in dying
A hidden colour city
Only light years away

The Millennial Arrangement

An age
A dream
A time machine
A nameless face amongst the wreck
With nothing else alone to check

Beleaguered, believing
Enrapture less deceiving
Finite and phased out
Crab-spent and choked with doubt

Fitting the glove
And filling with love
Just not sure anyone else will see it

I weasel it out of songlines
Sulk phenobarbitone night times
Spelling it out
For all those prepared to listen

Cease and desist
Channelling the bliss
Quaint to the brain
And charmed by the sin
Relishing the explanation all the more

As the dragon comes knocking on my door
The knowing of what it's all for

Wanderlust

I'm west bound
Headin' o'er the ole Tambourine
Closer to the forest
And my soul needs a clean

Trustin' crusts of coasts
I can make the most
Of this dream

Synchronise this time
We'll be feelin' fine
What a great team

Wow, look at all this gold?
The colour in my heart has a hold
Been three months now on the road
And it ain't gettin' old

Take my hand, I'm sold

Now the water's lickin' my toes
Insects dancin' on my nose
The water's reflectin'
This lifetime resurrection
And where we off to next?

Who would know?

At Our Suggestion

The feathers are humming
Falling in dreamtimes
And right times
To make you see
And make you free

The daring persuasion
Of spiritual salvation
Declaring itself
With lost cause damnation
But you crave complexities
And question what's next
For thee?

Tear drum and hind-tartened
The relatives smartened your need

For who would you be
Without crisp sentiment
A diary entente
Sincere sentient
For your familial season

Makes you feel tall
To stand strong for all
You identify
Even though you cry

And in your heart's mind
You seek to define
The pestilence
And rogue desistance

But who looks too deeply
Out of whim?
The family program
Is not a sham

And who would suggest it?

You're Family Now

They came from a sore point of quarters
Happy in seeming
Contentedly dreaming
Harmonising the philly's promotion

Setting up parcels
Forever unwrapping
Streamlining their hellbent devotion

Criteria mixed
With apparent position
Delicious on the outside
Tasty in the middle

Their love swore expletives
Bottling all the riddles
Swan song suggestive
Everyone cheered, hurray!

Goddess defined, happy days

The beautiful daughter we've raised
He seems so very deserving
A life that's worth pursuing
Patterning and no less unnerving
Proving the pleasantries perving

If one could not see
To the other degree
It smelt like their fame
Was still serving

Quick to besmirch
Yet praise all it's worth
Difficult cuddles
Plastered politeness
Digging up dirt
To find depth in their rightness

Knowing the thrill to receive them
Was courted in damnedest believing

The wisdom in beauty
And the will to be happy
Western division
Triumphed ablution
Making this vessel a home
Where only the select few may roam

Blustered in blisters
Convincing the sisters
That free time doesn't come quite so free

Taxed to the max
And driven by rhymes
Plato relaxed
Dusty defined

Bio transitions
Spare cent collection
What exactly is it
We're saving for?

We've all gotta rock n' roll sometime, she
swore

Or so the fisherman boasted
And clearly the decision was toasted
So they went about business
And met on the way

Some dainty point desistance
Assistance with listlessness
Through historical tested display

But the craft meant persistence
The virgin array
Familial resistance
Found at ease on that day

Made of Stars

    I celebrate
    Not the time
    Or the space
    But the memories I can't erase

    A long past reflection
    Of moments that have existed
    Steeped in the celebration
    Of who we each are

    A bright, shiny star

Psychic Sway

Do I ask that you believe with me?
Do I ask that you deceive with me?
Epic transgressions of human proportions
Are delivering me with pure intentions

This silly suggestion
It's out of the question
But your frilly boots
Keep me distracted

Occupied
Blind-sided
And familiarly fried

For all the ridiculous tears I've cried
I'm taking time and wasting mine
Communicating with everything I find

Test me as you rest me
Batteries and blessed be
I quest unto the Nile
And frolic in the style
Devotion outdating notions
That come back in a while

The effervescent
And ever-present
Are requesting an audience
With primal ascendants

Clear the floor
They're wanting more
Can't you feel them too?

You think I'm wasting time
And basting mine
But I'll meet you soon I know

Cracks in toes
No one else knows
The pathway spirit shows

A Prayer for Claire

In a dream
I carried you with me
I lifted you up
And took away your pain

The healing
Was a river of power
That floated down
From the stars

You glittered
And you glowed
As angels surrounded you
Dancing in the light
Shining from within you

You were luminous and bright
As bright as any star
There was no room for fear
There was no room for dark

The power of your essence
Shocked me to my core
Spellbound as I lay witness
In the realms of evermore

Each blast of beautiful light
The echoes of your laughter
The sweetness of your sing-song
Heaven's fair-hearted daughter

The magic in your wake
Filling up all space
As fireworks of energy
Radiated through this place

Pure love and divine bliss
Clearly seeing you through
For God's illustrious daughter
There was nothing more I could do

Safe in the arms of the holy
The stars never seemed so bright
The heaven's resounding loudly
As another earth angel takes flight

The One's Who

Messages to no one
In a world of nothingness
Arms worn bare
On an arm chair

No one may notice
Some master's apprentice
So quick to quip
On a bright, summer's day

With empty threats
And loaded guns
So bothersome to the heavens
So essential all the same
To a time of knowing

Circle around
Like the dancing hands
On the face of time
As graceful as lovers
Of the moon

Circling back
Circling back
Too soon

Their words drip like tears
On the open wounds
Of their souls

Their heartache rendered
With each open gash administered
The gulf of darkness widening
To split the world in two

The one's who will not
From the one's who

All I Ask

Oh, grant me this
Just one thing
I beg of thee
To help me sing

I beg of ye
Help my soul take flight
Through yonder stars
That light up the night

I tread o'er rock
And bracken fern
Seeking sweeping vistas
And yearning for more

I catalogue the details fair
Unloading each persuasion
Of home

Dismantle, dissect
But wish the best
For each poor soul
Put to the test

We rummage through
Piles and piles
As our feet still wander
Miles and miles

In footfalls ancient
In their score
The place where spirits
Rupture and soar

"What be your pleasure?"
Of course they ask

"Just help me sing"
It's all I ask

Pepe

Pepe couldn't take it anymore
The stench of death
Was burning his nostrils
His heart was ready
To explode
With the pain
Of loss

He stumbled out of the house
And without thinking
Blindly followed the path
That led deep into the forest

He stumbled forward
Tears stinging his eyes
As he fiercely drove them away
With a clenched fist

The pain!
Oh, the heartache
The storm in his soul
That threatened to drown him out
To wash him away

A plague on no one's house!
Who could even wish it?
He could never wish this hurt
On his worst enemy

The haphazard loss
The futile hope
The threads clung to
Gone threadbare
As another life is lost
Now another

Oh, piteous, odious sight
Oh, blight of eyes seen
That can never be unseen
Wife
Mother
Son
Daughter

No more, he begged
Knowing not to who

No more

He careened forward
Along the rocky path
Twilight taking hold
Of the darkening forest
Tripping over rock and tree root
Noticing little
Caring even less

If he did . . .
If he fell . . .

Suddenly his thoughts gathered

What if he did?
What if his brains were dashed
Against a rock
And the kiss of death
Graced his lips?
That would be it
He could escape

He could be free

Maybe if he couldn't find
The misstep he needed
Maybe the sheer drop
Off a cliff . . .

His focus sharpened
It may have to be

Perhaps death
Would be the only hope
For a pitiable soul
Surrounded by death

Suddenly, he halted

He stood dumbfounded
Shocked into awareness

A light, hovering in his path
A bright, dancing, luminous light

And there she was
Lighting up the path
Hovering right there
Right before him

A faery!
A tiny, glowing nymph
Of beauteous, joyful light!

Pepe sunk to his knees
Wondering whether
What his eyes were witnessing
Could possibly be true
Or were they certainly
Deceiving him?

'She's right here in front of me!
She seems so real!'

He sat dumbfounded
And couldn't help himself
He outstretched his hand
Hoping to touch the vision
This magical indecision
That was threatening to
Overwhelm and undo him

That was threatening
To fill him
With love and hope
Once more

Leaving Home

Clever being
Aren't you a chook?
How does it feel
To take a new look?

Craze it out
Haze away
Come up shining
New to play

Resting your choices
Cleft unto be
Standing in voices
That can't wait to see

You're leaving the burrow
Wait till it's done
Come all tomorrow's
Have none but fun

The choice is yours
Make it some

The Mystery

Not much more
Could I express
Any other way

The night, the cloud
The majesty of solitude
In the glimpse of greatness

Unrecognizable
To the eyes
Of a humbled woman
A stumbled woman
A crumpled woman

Each page never written
Each time never played
Each curse never earned
Each blessing never burst

For want of a constant motion
To always be here

To create my own mystery
Receiving the power
That was always meant for me

Burn Anew

Crying poor
When I have no excuse
The wealth in my mind and body
The gifts given
And the kindest ability
To put things into action

My kind of things

I speak in poetry
Because I've forgotten my voice

But what about
When I remember love?
That divine intervention
That has me running
And skipping
And yahooing
Into the sunset and beyond

Feeling out the stars
The mountainous moons
That called me
And I came galloping
Across the way
Just to catch a glimpse
And feel my body sway
To a newer state of me

That release of being
That raucous state of knowing
The beauty of what's in store
And feeling the passion
Burn anew

This must be my aim in life now

The Lucky Country?

Would you ever pick it?
A truth laid bare
Like a naked babe
Emanating a belief
Struck deep from the grief
Of a well-thought out plan
To better our land

Stand out from the rest

Australia
Clearly the best
Beset by the luckiness
That works us so

Never trust to let it go
In our nation
Our land
The notion
That we will
Stand divine

Like a Prayer

What will it take
To open this door?
To ask for more
And still be unsure
Of what the future brings

She sings it daily
Like a prayer

But when she dances
The shadows move
Without a trace
And let her past

If she could be there daily
What she wouldn't give

So what will it take?

The Artist's Movement

Golden seal

The artist's movement
Was clear to all
Maybe less so
To her

Come off it!
She's doing it deliberately!
Look at her
She's playing it up!

She must know
She's got something special

But the eyes boring into her
Were nothing new
And triggered little concern

Whatever taunt she possessed
Was a byline
To a will that held her

It beheld her
She felt it's presence
Her target audience

These folks were lovely
But inconsequential

Well, not completely so
Where would she be
Without the inspiration of others?

She needed the company
The reflection
The information on par
That came with the studying
Of another

The endless fascination
Of an entire human entity

But she didn't need to impress them
Maybe a little, at times
Undoubtedly sometimes a lot

But her life was her work
And with each move
A practice
Practising existence

A telephone ring and a call?
She could ignore it, wholeheartedly
Never ever, though
Could she ignore the call of spirit

The tantalising flavour
A special viewing
Who has come tonight
To watch the show?

The artist's movement became
So clear to her now
But maybe less so to all

The Cautious Cancer

Open my heart
From the dead inside
Cheer me when
I make my move

My stance for a positive change
A giant leap
Giant steps for a little one
Who wants to see the stars

Why are you so scared?
For the defiled steps
We pay in laymen

I know I don't
Understand you enough
But you are
Will you
Let me learn

How can they possibly
Understand, right?

Deuteranopia
The most cautious cancer
Of our time

Don't Look Back

Don't breathe in
And don't hold your breath
For you may never hear it coming
Danger on the tracks

Your soul
Bound and gagged
Tag me a fool
Of the vilest kind

When I was young I knew
When I was older I knew
But when it came to you
That's when I turned my back

Laid my life
Down on that track
Just to feel the hurt
Run me right over

Did you ever wonder
How much we could take
Here down under?

Before the night rains closed in
And we opened our doors
No more

Only to be sure
That the thing that was true
Was our solitude

No rude cuff
Will break our back
We'll just stay here
On this track

Don't worry, Lord
We won't look back

The Running Show

This is more than a story
It's a dialogue
Between two lost friends
Who fought
To find their way back

Upper hand is grasped
By a willing contender

Debts laid bare
For lifetimes done

A chance to change
And feel brand new
In a modern time

Praising the past

The lessons learned
And ghosts laid to rest
To bring us back into
A running show

Burning old bushes
Planting new seed
Regenerating love
For the highest source
Of reality

No longer afraid
Of what was done

Inviting one another
To come and be
To wait and see

For the future story
Wanting to be told
Set in bloodlines
And sparkling fray

Ever the promise
Of a neon day

The Baptism

Sold out on broken feelings
Aching body and mind
My soul is sore
With all the effort it takes
Just to hate you

For what?
You don't love me
Can't get blood from a stone

I must learn to let go
Fists unclench
Baptized with razor blades
Hatred bleeds away

Life is cleansed
I gently drift down
Falling in love
With me again

My soul is soaring
Can't change us
Can't change you
But I can change me
And I can forgive

Now I'm free

The Wait

Brakes are
A temporary intervention
Of an ethereal disconnection

Don't wait too long
But you'll wait a lifetime
Cause you're strong

American Creek

Let's go down to the waterhole
Let's go down to the creek
Let's drink from the waterhole
Let's drink from the creek

American Creek
American Creek

Look up at Keira
Look up at the stars
Look up at Djembla
The mountains stretching so far

American Creek
Down by American Creek

The burning land around us
Burning spirits and the reigning hand
The death cries and the land ties
Take whatever you can

From American Creek
American Creek

Roll yourself another cigarette
It's gonna take some time
200 years to finally realise
What's yours and what's not mine

All around American Creek
And every other creek

Slowly poisoning the waterholes
Waging war on every black heart
Trickling blood, raging torrents, a deathly
                river
Cursing the land, a crippling place to start

Down around American Creek
And every other creek

The long-forgotten beauty ghostly
                glimmers
The hope of healing in the night
As I pray to all the spirits around me
That the ancestors never give up the fight

To save American Creek
And every inch of this land we seek

American Creek
The beauty of American Creek
The history of American Creek
The rotten story we never speak

All began near American Creek

The Traveller

Who are you mate?
You look cool
Which fool
Counselled your company?

Maybe a twitch
In paydirt
But I had my foot
On the back peg
The whole way

So how do you know
Until you try?

Cause where you feel
The tension
Did I mention
A quick trip?

Up a dynamic
Vert
Rugged
Stepped
Treed
And planted path

Way up
To the tippy top
Of a wee mountain

Hey baby, let's go

Acknowledgements

As I have meandered through life, I have left a great many friendships hanging in limbo, purely as logistics would dictate, the difficulty in keeping in contact with so many beautiful souls on a regular basis is just impossible when I have travelled so much and lived around different parts of Australia. When social media came along, it changed all of this – but only to the point where you can see your loved ones, you can't always get to them.

Thank goodness we even had that through our version of the Roaring 20's – the Boring 20's. Covid, lockdowns, homeschooling . . . a bevy of supremely shite days, made light by the wonderous sight of our loved ones on a screen.

To Nigel Parker, one of my high school mates, who was one of those people that, thanks to social media, I had the chance to reconnect with, although our paths did cross with a frequency that made me acutely aware of how much I cared for the bloke, a genuine, funny, thoughtful, intelligent and prime example of masculinity in all of its beautiful nuances – my heart goes out to all of his loved ones, and to all of my high school friends who I know will be missing him dearly. RIP mate.

Kylie, Ange, Sharon, Nicole, Bronwen, Dene, Dee, Nikki, and all of the rest of you Stawell peeps, note well how much I love you, and how I wish I could see more of you to reminisce and make new memories, but please know how grateful I am just to see your beautiful faces on the screen – it's the next best thing to a dream come true.

Beautiful Rosie (and her angels), Sue, Nellie, Gina, Alecia, Lou, Katie, Ange, Lis (Mrs H), Del, Jo, Veronica, Shaun, Heather, Bec and all of the other magical cheer champs who I don't get to see but are always quick with a funny or a beautiful comment, it makes the days worthwhile, thank you!

To my brother Robbie, my sis Amanda, and my sister-in-laws Treesh and Carls, thanks for all of the love and support.

To Gavaaaawwwn (sorry mate, I couldn't resist), cheers and beers for all of the horty lorfs and inspiratiaaaawwwn.

Frank and Kel, thank you beyond words for all of the magical moments that have fuelled happy memories, that have bonded our families and have marked time in ridiculously fun and special ways – "Keep writing and you will keep inspiring," bloody hell Frankie, I'll never forget!

There are others, I can't mention everyone but I love your time in my life, please know that.

Last but not least, to all of my goddesses, gods and guides, guardian angels, mothers and fathers of the land, faery friends and magical spritely beings, thank you . . . thank you, thank you, thank you, thank you! Thank you.

About the Author

Catherine Harford is an artist, poet and writer living in Wollongong, south of Sydney, Australia, with her husband and her two children. Wollongong is Dharawal Country, the traditional lands of the Dharawal people and she honours their nation, both past, present and future.

She produces a variety of art, which includes music and video production as well as her penchant for drawing and painting – likewise she has been adding song writing to her growing collection of musings. She is the published author of "They Gave Me Truth" and the collection of poems, "Under Moon and Sun."

From a young age Catherine sought to dedicate her time to uncovering the true heartbeat of her nation, travelling extensively and absorbing as much of the landscape and the psyche of her grand, island country as possible.

Australia is a deeply divided nation, in both its history and its sense of identity. From the machinations of a fast-paced and generally forward-thinking city life, to the laid-back, beautiful yet often-times staid determination of life in the country, there is a deep wound that affects everyday living in so many parts of this wide, brown land. Ignorance of history, potent racial tension and an arduous dedication to commercial progression has done great damage, physically, psychically and mentally, to the Australian people, whether they are collectively aware of it or not.

The indifference to the suffering of Australia's ancient Aboriginal people, and their spiritual connection with, love of and fierce care for the land is slowly, slowly, so slowly being bought to light, and steps are gradually being taken to rectify this pitiful wounding which has occurred throughout the invasive white chapter of Australia's history. Catherine has a deep-seated conviction that until Indigenous Australians are honoured and treated with the reverence they deserve, that the restless, seeking spirit of this suffering shall haunt all Australians, until a deep healing finally takes place.

Having lived in this life of racial prejudice against both the oldest and the newest of Australians, as well as with the very real threat to the planet from humans with their voracious appetite for consumerism, Catherine made it her mission to not only heal her own self from the wounds she accrued through her own life story, but to discover a language that might inspire healing, from within the individual, from within the society and from within the bounds of energetic forces that connect us all as one – after all, Australia is just one country in our global village, and in so many of those villages, the need to act, to fast-track the healing process is crying out to be heard.

She hopes her words open people's minds, helps heal their souls and touches their hearts, and that they, too, will feel a movement toward a global connection in loving one another, the planet, and the spiritual realm that tirelessly guides us onwards, on this crazy journey called life on earth.

www.ingramcontent.com/pod-product-compliance
Lightning Source LLC
LaVergne TN
LVHW040055080526
838202LV00045B/3642